IN

ANDREW WATERHOUSE

IN

First published in 2000 by
THE RIALTO
PO Box 309, Aylsham, Norwich NR11 6LN
Re-printed 2002

ISBN 0-9527444-1-4

The publisher acknowledges financial assistance from the Esmee Fairbairn Charitable Trust and the Eastern Arts Board

Eastern Arts Board Funded

The Rialto is a Registered Charity No. 297553

Printed by Printing Services (Norwich) Ltd.

For Hala and Nina

ACKNOWLEDGEMENTS

Acknowledgements are due to the editors of the following publications in which some of these poems first appeared: *The Rialto, Smiths Knoll, The North, Cyphers, Other Poetry, Headlock, Frogmore Papers, Tears in the Fence, Red Herring, Ploughshare, The Crack, Iota, The Interpreter's House and Staple*. 'One Day in Late Adolescence' appeared in the *Forward Book of Poetry 2000* and was broadcast on Radio 4. A number of the poems also appeared in *Need-Fire* (Bay Press, 1996).

Andrew Waterhouse would like to thank Ian Patience, Linda France, Jo Shapcott, David Stephenson, Michael Laskey, Roy Blackman, Lluis and Cesca at the Centre D'Art I Natura, and the staff at the Tyrone Guthrie Centre: thanks also to Northern Arts for a Writer's Award in 1997

CONTENTS

You breathe in, you breathe out,
You breathe in, you breathe out,
You breathe in, you breathe out,
You breathe in, you breathe out.

Van Morrison
"Beside You"

ONE DAY IN LATE ADOLESCENCE

It being suggested that I get out of myself more,
I get out of the family home and into low cloud.
A door bangs behind me and here lies North Marsh Road
and December, where the lamps have been on all day.
Adjacent, there may be a town, tidal river, power station;
but this view is cut to pavement and a Maestro browning nicely.
Also, the aged appear, trolleys pulling them home.
They breathe heavily, making their own winter.

At the crossroads I wait for a lorry dribbling sand,
then straight over past The House of Close Relations,
but I will not call being sick of myself and all others.
To the right are allotments where my father buries
something most days. Note the freshly turned earth,
hear the pigeons mumbling about the sun and spilt grain.

And now a sharp rise, up the embankment and I look down
upon the weighty Trent, brown, see the whirlpools eating
themselves and a barge grows from the fog, slips around the bend,
bearing coal to Hull and even beyond. It disappears,
making a wake I must follow, which is where I will leave myself,
hunched and walking by a river in December,
hoping that one day I will return in human form.

NOT FINDING A PASSAGE OR THE SOURCE OF ANYTHING

There was much rejoicing in the city,
as they set off in fine weather,
wearing safari suits and stiff white shirts.
At the edge of the jungle the camera crews
turned back. The explorers walked on,
but soon outdistanced their maps.
The bearers deserted, so they took
on the weight themselves, redistributed it equally
and continued cutting through the undergrowth.

One morning the radio weakened
and talked thereafter only in a language
with which they were not familiar.
The boat began taking in water.
It had been built in the vernacular,
of vine leaves stretched over the ribcage
of a whale. It was an accurate reconstruction
from old texts, but not seaworthy.
Waves broke upon them from a great height.

By the third month they had forgotten
their Fine Purpose. They examined
the equipment that remained, seeking clues,
but found only a number of tape measures
and a glass ball. They met no other humans alive,
but noted bodies floating face down in the swamp.
They dragged out as many as they could,
gave them a Christian burial,
then moved quickly on.

Water supplies ran low.
Under a desert sun, they drank urine,
but only their own. They ate
their shoes, beards and the dogs.
Their extremities were reabsorbed;
counting became problematical and they lost
track of the days. Three of the party
were presumed dead, having been gone for some time.
The remainder became conscious of their own bones.

The efforts of rescuers were hampered
by rough sea and low cloud.
To them it was just another job
and they would not work in the rain.
The government refused to comment. Interest
at home faded. The faces of the travellers were cut
from school photographs, wives remarried, daughters
wrote disturbing biographies. All hope was mislaid.
Mail was no longer forwarded.

Towards the end, the explorers
made little progress, preferring instead to follow
their own footprints in the snow.
They heard the ice crack, felt it shift
beneath their feet. On the final day they gathered
together for warmth, taking turns on the outside.
They reclaimed friendship, told stories
of their fathers and childhood, watched a fine sun
set and waited for its return.

LOOKING FOR THE COMET

You push back the sheet, leave me
naked and cooling in the night air.
You stand by the window,
by the yellow flowers in their blue vase
and there's moon on your face and shoulders.
"It's here," you say, but I'm pretending sleep,
and just watch you, watching the comet
moving off towards the sun and beyond.

A car passes. Headlights fill the window,
making new shadows, that rise, then fall.
You take a flower from the vase,
carry it to me in both hands, slowly wipe
the petals over my face. Now, I can smell
the pollen on my skin, feel the trail.

AN ORCHARD TRUCE

(Kibbutz En Hashofet, August 1978)

Full of red, head weighted against reason,
I float in this maternal pool,
water still thicker and warmer than blood.
Beyond the diving board a fringe of hills
and closer in towers above the wire
our guards crouch. They are right to be watchful.
This peace may fail.
            I kick out, glide from shallows
to the deep. I remember the day's apples,
fat and hard on the tree; my unsteady ladder
disappearing through leaves to crisp grasses,
where snakes coil and recoil.
            The present breeze
brings resin, a needle scatter and she
steps down from celebrations, pauses unseeing
by the edge, slips off her dress. Blackened skin
swallows moonlight, arching over stars,
knifing the water. A fine arrival.
I hope that she will surface by my shadow.

NOT AN ENDING

He never lived in that valley
or anywhere else. On the night in question
he did not stand by the river or ignore
the new rain or drop stones into the water.
There were no tree songs around him,
no unidentified birds, no flowing to the sea.

Her eyes were not blue. Those were not her boots.
She walked more quickly. He did not hear
her last word or want to. He may
have shrugged, but never shook.
He had no regrets and would not think
of her again. He would not think of her again.

A NIGHT AT THE PLAGUE AND NAUSEA

(Winter, 1996)

I

Forced out of my house by the Great Cold,
I walk white fields to the blond person
behind the bar. I say: "We'll all be dead soon"
and she laughs as she pours. I stare at her face:
the careful red. Money is passed back. She remarks:
"We can never truly know each other or anyone else."

II

Sitting by the fire, I admire its realism;
the jugs, much leather and polished brass.
She replaces my drink, leans over, whispers:
"Everything is meaningless. You know I'm right."

III

Many hours pass. I sway by the door,
listening to the snowfall. The bell sounds
behind me. I smile, free to decide:
a last request or the white fields.

IN

1. The Forest at Night

This is a forest.

Here is a car
in the forest.

That is a person
in the car
in the forest.

This is a quiet forest.

THE NEED-FIRE

...the peasants in many parts of Europe have been wont from time immemorial to resort to a ritual fire at irregular intervals in seasons of distress and calamity...
Sir James Fraser, *The Golden Bough*

This can be recommended; an alternative to Prothiaden
and community workers. It has a proven record
against murrain at least and a wide application
in our present state.
First, extinguish all flames
and sparks in the night. Dowse the streetlights,
the hand-held torches, the glow of the microwave.
Bring two oak logs from the forest behind
the supermarket. Let nine times nine
first begotten sons (for they are the finest of all sons)
rub the rough timbers, grain against grain,
until they smoke and flare. Then light the pyre,
that which was prepared earlier. Attend the blaze
and let its smoke obscure the rising moon.
Presently, when the fire calms, bring out the sick
and corrupted. Encourage them over the embers.
Each parish can choose such favoured ones.
They may be unwaged, fallen women, the travelling people,
Moslems, homosexuals and other carriers,
the non-limbed, melancholics; any person who is not
of our pure stock. Walk them through the fire,
until their faces are blackened. Some may stumble
and be trampled. Let them rest. Those that live
shall be cured and made grateful. They will receive
a certified, flaming brand to rekindle their hearths.
They will take ashes to spread on their streets
against vermin and theft.
In this way, our society
shall be well cleansed and made new as we near
the millennium, as we suffer in our time of trouble.

ANOTHER POEM ABOUT THE END OF THE WORLD

Birds refuse to sing, even at dawn, even for the cameras.
They return to last summer's nests tight-beaked, crouch.
Safe eggs form around them. In a black case my favourite
red butterfly is drinking its own wings, becomes molten.
The hare slowly blinks from its perfect hollow, looks away
as I pass. There are pollen clouds flowing through
half-dismantled webs, past the tree refolding its leaves;
flowing back to the grasses of the summer plain, that yellow,
withdraw roots, let the soil loose to dance.

Meanwhile, we sit in darkened rooms, make conversation,
watch our volunteers at work. They paint the river bed blue,
but the stones are hot, will never dry. They inflate clouds
and release them from hilltops. Also, my aunt has recycled
her second husband. Also, I buy a low energy personality,
but it is too late. The weather is quickening to a gale
blowing sand from continent to continent, filling our mouths,
our industrial estates. We fall gasping as the grains build up,
making dunes of us all by the risen ocean. And afterwards,
there may be something of a silence, a natural pause;
until the fresh rain, germination, inhuman celebration.

THE WIFE'S STATEMENT

With hindsight I remember a growing silence,
the static quality of his last few months
spent crouched on that hillside in the rain.

"I'm weathering," he said indistinctly, his mouth full
of pebbles and would not come home to wash.
His hands were lichened. There were crystals on his cracked lips.

All that summer, the heather crawled up around him.
Mosses feathered his naked back. "I've discovered
the fossil within," he claimed one morning

and never touched the food I left.
He was slipping well below ground,
until only his upturned face remained,

letting rain collect and freeze in his eyes,
catching the light for that final whispering:
feldspar, mica, quartz, feldspar, mica, quartz.

PATHETIC FALLACIES AT CORRIMONY ANCIENT MONUMENT, INVERNESS

It's raining when we arrive.
The sky is the greyest I have
ever seen. We walk through puddles.
There is a large heap of grey stones

which have been grey for some time.
You find the middle tomb,
sit in its dark, hugging your knees.
You will be thinking of birthings

and solstices, other forms
of social organisation, other relations.
A cloud shifts, here is the sun
and you smile. Various birds begin

to call. You smile at what
you have found by accident at last,
touch each boundary stone,
each orange lichen.

It's raining as we leave.
Our car is the greyest I have
ever seen. We need to talk again.
I say this to the windscreen.

IN

2. Cup

They gave me a drink
and asked me the name of our monarch.
The cup was badly cracked.
The monarch was unwell.

They nodded when I spoke,
because I was polite and being wise;
then took my belt and laces.
They made me welcome.

THE DEPUTY UNDER-CHAMBERLAIN SPEAKS OF THE FIRST TIME HE SAW LADY SEI SECHONG IN THE PALACE GARDENS

During and after the forty-fifth second
of the third quarter
of the Hour of the Snake
on the twelve day
of the God-Frozen Month
in the seventh year
of the Elder Sister of Fire
Stroking the Muzzle of the Rat
and, friends, I should have known better.

NOW THE CITY HAS FALLEN

The radio station is filled with goats,
all telephone lines recoiled to their source,
the city gates closed and locked for the last time.

Women are shackled and painted red,
the men given false beards and new names;
I am *He Who Looks Nervously Behind,*
my friend is *He Who Looks Nervously Above.*
They want us all to be very nervous.

The first born of a first born has to give
an organ to God. The rich buy poor men's livers
from secret markets. There is never a shortage.

All trees are being felled as they keep heaven
from earth. The invaders eat only human flesh
Our children are taken from us and reared
in darkness. It is unclean to wash the body,
only the soul can be touched and scoured bright.
It must be left out on the roof tops
for the sun and moon. This is the law.

TRAVEL UPDATE FOR A BUSY KINGDOM

Overnight, a heavy fall
of infants. Roads blocked.
Our Social Service does all
it can, but the children refreeze,

are treacherous. Due to unseasonal gravities
walking now possible only for the slim.
A plague on the nation's airports.
Red underwing pustules. They

burst. Engines also are swelling.
Flight abandoned until cured.
In tunnels, rails curl to the touch,
make letters, but it is too dark to read.

You may not arrive. Our thin monarch's final appeal:
"Stay at home my people. Sit. For once, be still."

TWENTY (INCLUDING DOUBLE WORD SCORE)

Thanks to LJ

After their dessert,
they play by candlelight,
stars and a moon he made earlier.

She is well-painted,
his moustache freshly waxed.
They may not be young, but are hopeful.

There are half-smiles,
quarter-glances, stray hands
almost touch on a glass. Then gently, but firmly

on the *o* of her *ovules*
he lays *throb*, leans close,
breathes: "It could have been *broth*."

IN

3. TV

Evening in the lounge and also on a distant planet.
We sit: yellow sky, ringed moons and shadows
on the rocks of the surface. There has been
an encounter and counsellor Troi is beautiful,
but surrounded. She reports to Picard: "Captain,
I sense confusion, low self-esteem and denial.
The aliens are angry, but mean us no harm. I believe
we can help them." She is right and I am relieved,
nod my three heads, want to tell her everything.

BINARY

(for Kruger 60, in the constellation of Cepheus)

I say: "According to my *Collins Pocket Guide*
*to the Universe**, most stars are mated.
They will differ in utter luminosity,
total spectral type and absolute magnitude,
but share a common gravity. They may even shed
mass to each other."

You say nothing, smile, turn a page.

Later that same evening, I feel the fire
between us subsiding and move closer.
It is the year's end. We are running
low on fuel. No wonder I worry
about implosions, about who will be the red giant.

**2nd edition, over 100 sky charts and photographs*

DISSATISFIED LIFE FORMS (1-4)

1
A bear and the sun going down
and the bear sniffing the air
and scratching at the tree,
whispering: "Help me out
of this skin and under your bark.
I will stand in the rain forever
and never kill again."

2
Forty something starfish on the phone
to his cosmetic evolutionist:
"I have a surfeit of legs. Do something.
The vertebrates are mocking me."

3
A pastel room. Two comfortable chairs,
a low table, tissues. An amphibian sits,
other life form listens, feels his pain:
"You know, it's really weird, sometimes
I just feel like a princess inside."

4
Brother moth completes
his final journal entry:
the dark, the dark.
Flies up, turns,
gathers speed
towards the whitest light.

IN A NEARBY DIMENSION

"Love" means to keep clean
and in a resaleable condition.

What is furthest is largest,
for example planets. To speak

I make words into liquids,
pass them from my mouth

to your mouth. You should keep
to the low ground as our gravity

is presently unreliable. A stranger
would not want to see your husband's face.

We believe in our ancestors
and that they live on in the white goods

of the family. A question
can be asked, but not answered.

This would suggest a completion
and be impolite. We believe

in the redistribution of disease.
Please leave without speaking.

Return all gifts. We are honest
and care for each other.

STRAVSKA: LAND OF GRACE AND GRANDEUR

Visitor, you are welcome! Indeed we are most fond
and open our country, handicrafts and hearts to you.
This land may be small, but is highly coloured
and with virginity unmatched from the snow heights
of tectonic masses to the dozing plain rivers,
strolling and indirect.
            Climatologically, national insolation
values (both spring, summer and autumn)
are respected and precipitive incidents fall lightly
throughout the touristic season. We therefore invite
the enjoyment of our industrio-cultural complexes;
please stroll the museums, the concentrated camps
(now restored) and our ethnographic reservations;
enjoy the bullock masks, painted brides, the weaving
of butter and scratched bones. Drink! Eat!
Stravskan broth has overfilled many, flesh is widely
to hand and our red most jocular.
            To the effectual
we advise: defeat the mountains, shoot our wolves
and boars, trot and gallop, be pedalling, bird gaze
and angle. Respectfully, we invite the indisposed
to be corrected, for we have thermal waters hot
and spicy. If your skin is disordered or any organ
enigmatic then you shall be assisted with pain.
                Friends,
may you unearth great delight in our savoury land
now speeding on the autobahn of gratuitous endeavour.
Join us on this fine journey. Prices are negotiable.

WHY OUR SACRED TREE WEARS NO SANDALS AND WHY THE MOON SOMETIMES SMILES

Having sat with silence for a wife,
on a sharp stone we call *The Sharp Stone*,
on the mountain we call *The Mountain*
for thirty days and thirty nights,
without food, or water or his mule;
he spoke and it was in his voice used
for the shining truths we call
The Shining Truths and also urgent
personal requests and we drew close and listened:

"Beloved children, hear my words:
I have sat with silence as my wife
on *The Sharpest Stone of the Mountain*
for thirty days etc., without food,
or water, or my mule for comfort and so on
and so forth. And children I have seen many visions,
have been tempted by the unnamed devils
who cannot be named, laughed with the rock
as it weathered, cried with the full moon
as it fell to the plain and I say this:
there was once a time before footwear
when we walked directly upon the earth
and so grew tall and strong as brothers
and sisters to all things and I have seen
that time and it was most beautiful
and will be so once again."

And after the saying of this, he took off
his sandals, pushed his feet into the dry earth,
until each toe extended, curled, became a root;
he held his arms up to *The Sharp Stone
of the Mountain* and they became branches,
grew leaves and flowers and fruits and birds
that sang. He smiled and his beautiful smile
rose up into the sky and became the young
and old moon that watches over his children.

IN

4. Nightmare

Not seen, felt.
A pressure on my chest;
stones, potatoes, love, moonlight,
a blanket, white ash and guilt.
And who is this, standing at the root
of the bed, breathing beer, adding more weight;
until with a small sound the ribs split apart.

BEHIND A BAR

It being the quiet time. Fires lit.
Glasses polished. Bottles dusted,
turned label first and my father
exercises his mind, lifting words

like weights from the book:
enero, febrero, marzo and on, a whole year
passing slowly in a country he may
not visit and here is a regular

needing a small half and ready salted.
"Buenos tardes," my father smiles,
exhibits a small flamenco shuffle
which has taken much practise.

The regular nods, carries his drink
and large silence to the fire,
where it is beyond any heat
and my father now opening

the hatch to his cellar, looking up,
"Tu eres una silleta,"*
descending to find more work,
"Senorita, me ha dado el numero equivocado."**

**You are a bed pan*
***Operator, you have given me the wrong number*

NIGHT POEM

My mother and father in the dark,
having heard news of a late frost.
My father crouching to the ridges,
pulling soil over stiffening leaves,
my mother trying to hold the light steady;
around them the silent town,
a clearing sky, the colder air.

THE BODY BY TORCHLIGHT

Your shadow leant on our home.
I have always lived under it.
During gales I feared you,
but in summer there was shade
and much singing.

I watched your slow failure;
the scalded leaves,
a retreat from edges,
bone timber with its beetle tattoo.
My childhood fears returned,
made me pace your distances,
imagine trajectories.
I was not reassured.

Finally, you became useful again;
a valued habitat for birds
and animals without name.
You welcomed the bearding lichens,
looked your best in moonlight;
bats on wires among the simplified canopy.

Until that is, the last storm
laid you across the grass,
woke me from a patricidal dream.
I examined the body by torchlight,
pronounced it dead, was not relieved.

LOCHAN

Off the track, over infirm peat,
juniper, a heather fringe
and then the pool, having settled
years before, water always wanting
to make more of itself;
if only to show clouds, sky patches,
a range of grey
                and now the sun,
breeze, waves pushing south
towards the lowlands, a rise and fall
of surfaces, of sheen
                and at depth
still the touch of old ice unchanged,
black water thickening
to mud around stumps and rocks.

IN

5. Soup

I don’t know the man opposite;
a new arrival, dark, but familiar. He says:
“Yesterday, brother, I had my stitches out”

and casually takes his hand off his throat
to show me the rough line flecked with scabs,
the skin stretching as he swallows.

Smiling, he tears at the bread,
holds it down in the soup with his spoon.

BURNING YOUR BROTHER'S GUITAR

You may have a brother; if not imagine one who gave you
his guitar, at a forgotten time, for an unknown reason.
Suppose that this guitar has travelled with you from house
to safe house, always left in darkness under a bed
in the sparest room. Recall that your brother's guitar
which became yours, was well beyond tuning, the action too high
for comfort, the varnish dull, scratched, pitted. All chords
were lost.

Suppose that you could not discard your brother's
guitar until after midnight January 1st 1989, when drunk,
needing warmth, with no party in sight, you pulled your brother's
guitar from the darkness under the bed in your sparest room.
Remember, that you stamped down hard, snapping the neck,
crushing the body, then threw the pieces of your brother's guitar
on the fire. Assume that the strings curled in the flames,
as if touched, touched privately and that you slept
on the floor in the heat until morning, then prodded
the ashes; grateful for the honest, precious metal
that remained after you had burnt your brother's guitar.

BEFORE THE HUNT

Fast for six weeks. Abstain from strong women and liquor.
Rub your flesh with briars, shells. Be continent Confess
your sins. Clean your dugout. Cast aside your umbrella.
Pray in the four corners of the municipality. Cut your body,
insert peppers and spices, sit in the sun until browned.
Gird the loins of a brother with Pandanus leaves
and he will do likewise. Polish your sandals. Sharpen
your moustache. You are a man. You are ready.

WATERSTONES IN THE SPRING

It being morning in the basement
and there is music, maybe
baroque and I am in *Biography*,
searching. At her post the assistant

who could be writing a letter to a lover
or the last draft of something
more significant and in front of her
a bearded man, rehearsing

his lines, arms slack, looking down. He speaks.
Wants a book on ambulances of the world.
There is nothing listed. He is told;
his left hand clenches, unclenches, clenches

and I move quickly to *Mind and Spirit*, hoping to find
us all the right crystal, karmic path, healing field.

THE MAN WHO GAVE UP EVERYTHING

As a protest against the situation
in the city, he severed a finger
and used it to point at the soldiers.
When the firewood ran out
he flayed himself and wrapped
small children and pets in his skin.
A memory of his birth was auctioned
for the benefit of the Christian Brothers.
The smell of his hair became a fragrance
sold in countries without forest.
I saw him smile for an artist
and stole his lips for my wife.
I heard him say *love* once
and took the word for myself.

IN

6. Ocean

There's waves.
You know,
waves.

And fish; fish in the water.
You know,
fish.

Salt. You can taste salt.

And here's a bird; big bird circling down,
wide wings, mouth open, coming down to the ocean.

You know,
ocean.

A DIFFICULT LANDING

She never flew, only in dream time,
when she forced a door, was sucked out;
her mother, father and brother following.
They tumbled through an atmosphere;
linked hands, formed a perfect unfamiliar square.

Going down, her father pointed out a passing eagle,
her mother smiled, her brother looked away.
They called to each other across gravity,
remarking on the sky's blueness and found time
to rediscover the view of trees, love and motorways
before they hit the ground; a hard place.

FIELD TRIP

First, geography:
    granite upland, settlement dispersed,
    a multiple choice of corries and arêtes,
    after ice, waterfalls work the hanging valleys.

Also ecology:
    you can use a quadrat to trap grasses,
    succession is just one thing after another,
    we all get a chance to see the snake under the stone.

Last, without syllabus:
    the shine of your wet hair,
    a hooded walk, attempting the summit,
    speaking in tongues in the black hall of the hostel.

THE CARDIGAN HAIKU: EXCERPTS FROM A SEQUENCE

From a distance, under the sun, a prostrate cardigan may look like an oasis. A Desert Proverb

I
Irksome cardigan;
held by your soft sleeves now,
as the sea ice melts.

VI
Up from the metro,
my cardigan traps petals.
The white faces shine.

XX
This morning after
the cardigan stinks of smoke.
Who was burnt last night?

XXIX
Deep in the wardrobe,
it was evening all day long,
no cardigan sang.

XXXVI
Cardigan pockets,
too full of flowers and glass
(yellow, purple, red).

XXXVIII
When the east wind blows,
cardigans without buttons
are of little use.

AN INVERTEBRATE STORY

(Why can't you pull yourself together?)

Along the littoral zone,
waves are breaking down.
From mother ocean
pools divide upon themselves,
collecting salt.
The tide is in withdrawal
again and much exposed,
which troubles molluscs and

I watch the unwise limpet
trail mucus from childhood
over granite, to find
the same depression:
familiar grind of rock and shell,
comfort of the home scar.

IN

7. Paper

Every session I paint the paper white,
all white, as white as I can make it,
like the white behind stars.

She asks me as the white dries:
"What do you feel about this whiteness?"
I continue, adding more white, whiter, whitest.

A CHOLERIC ABSTRACTION

Large, brightly-coloured;
sharp-edged when solid,
speaking only in Wolverine,
of true appetites. The scent
lingers, is hormonal, corditic.
You could lick the surface,
taste iron. There will always
be heat.

It is native and knows
the paths of our territory,
is quick to act in the forests
and at home. But, take care.
It does not sleep or forget
a face. It may save you
and disturb all relations,
happily raze your house
to the ground.

ROWAN*

Rocking to the touch, loose rooted in soured soil,
a struggle for grip. The trunk is split,
gash poorly healed. Leaves curl in September,
evading the wind. The blood is in the berries,
early and scarlet. This year could be the last,
a final excessive shedding onto heather
and hard fern, red and more red and more.

**Sorbus aucuparia*

Narrow crown, ascending branches. Twigs pubescent
when young, glabrous later. Lvs 10-25 cm, pinnate,
terminal equals lateral, serrated (sometimes doubly),
dark green above, sub-glaucous below.
Infl dense, anthers cream. Fr scarlet,
sub-globose, lenticels inconspicuous. Fl 5-7.
2n=n. MM or M.Woodlands, mountains. Short-lived native.

SELF-IMPROVEMENT

There is an evening outside
of sunlight, mowing and much blue.
I walk a corridor
passing the *Quaternary* and *Wittgenstein*.
Also the wine tasters of Provence
are becoming rowdy once again.

I am late.
The windows are open,
the pockmarked desks pushed back.
I join the circling around our teacher.
We breathe in,
breathe out,
balancing various energies.
There are certain movements to be enjoyed
without laughing. We:
          part a wild horse's mane,
          grasp a bird's tail,
          wave hands like clouds.
(Stevie is very cirrus, Benedict
so dark and full of old rain).
It is a slow business and I am elsewhere,
distracted by the distant calls of *North-East Birds*,
the faint scent of *Men's Thai Cookery (Intermediate)*.

Of course I am jealous
when Sharn spreads her wings,
when she becomes a white crane,
but I join the cheering
as she glides out
towards a conveniently setting sun.

MY FIREWOOD THERAPY

axe fall
catching light
what was one
is now two
blade halving
the bark
the bast
the xylem
cutting heartwood years
every slice thinning
as memory should
to a splinter
just beyond sight
to the final cell
my hand unsteady
wall now breached

organelles
spill out are lost
on the woodshed floor
no way back
but to cut
into the matrix
the cavities and membranes
the protein webs

breaking the long chains
towards a single molecule
to the lone atom
spinning in the dark

surrounded by uncertainty
still at the core

two particles to be split

IN

8. Window

On the window; a flower smeared
and four nurses come running.
He'd tried to break the glass
with his face or his face
with the glass, but only spread
blood on his lips, on his shirt
as they carried him out. He cried.

Now, the last of the sun, clouds,
abstract red on the window shining
and we could all be tested by that shape,
we could all say: rose, a sunset,
the sea, whatever you want, take us home.

THE SOFT PART OF THE ANIMAL

Underneath the scales,
thickened skin, shell, carapace;
full, red, still working.

COLLECTING THE KINDLING

(for Ruby)

Your daughter among the windfalls,
chattering to sticks,
choosing her favourite,
her very best friend
to pick, to drop,
as I fill the last bag with long dried elder.

She runs through the trees
and the weakening light,
away and close again,
now talking back to the rooks,
shouting down rabbit holes
and breathless takes my cold hand;
the small heat of her fingers.

TIRVIA, CATALONIA: THE LOST AFTERNOON

I watch a 4WD heading off to Andorra.
A wheelbarrow is taken for a walk.
Even in the shade of this lime tree,
three postcards are exhausting.
I need rest and another *San Miguel*.
The old men at the next table
are discussing home improvements
or the Civil War; making shelves
or removing someone's legs.
There is an argument. It must be
the shelves. Nothing happens for a while
and then again, until an unfocused leaf
falls from the tree, yellow, beautiful,
but reducing my shade. The wheelbarrow
is taken home drunk. The old men
have installed a jacuzzi or democracy.
After two more leaves, mother, I will go home,
find a wheelbarrow of my own.

CREATION OF THE WORLD (PLUS BREAKFAST)

Possibly an egg (unboiled, therefore delicate)
floated in the waters of that Big Moment.
It may have sung and cracked itself
or been smashed by a diving bandicoot.

Maybe a rock of the Sacred Mountain was split
into two by Our Mother of All Duality
or the Great Karmic Wind
blew an apple from the Tree of Life.

Perhaps a giant died, his sweat
became an ocean, his last breath
made clouds. Whatever. All things emerged
and were busy, which may explain

why we sit this morning in a June garden
with birdsong, sunlight and an egg to be cut.

LOWER PLANTS

Half-dark
under the canopy,
a careful place
of leaf fall
and webs,
where mosses
practise devotions
to clay,
steady rain
and moderation
in all things;
making secrets
of themselves
until the breeze
parts branches
for that moment
of allowed light:
jade, verdigris.
a shining.

IN

9. Snow

Filling the gaps between wards,
denying the existence of grass,
soil, the bedrock;

shaping tracks around the feet
of birds, which I follow
wanting to find their homes,
but always ending in mid-step,
making me look up.

CLIMBING MY GRANDFATHER

I decide to do it free, without a rope or net.
First, the old brogues, dusty and cracked;
an easy scramble onto his trousers,
pushing into the weave, trying to get a grip.
By the overhanging shirt I change
direction, traverse along his belt
to an earth stained hand. The nails
are splintered and give good purchase,
the skin of his finger is smooth and thick
like warm ice. On his arm I discover
the glassy ridge of a scar, place my feet
gently in the old stitches and move on.
At his still firm shoulder, I rest for a while
in the shade, not looking down,
for climbing has its dangers, then pull
myself up the loose skin of his neck
to a smiling mouth to drink among teeth.
Refreshed, I cross the screed cheek,
to stare into his brown eyes, watch a pupil
slowly open and close. Then up over
the forehead, the wrinkles well-spaced
and easy, to his thick hair (soft and white
at this altitude), reaching for the summit,
where gasping for breath I can only lie
watching clouds and birds circle,
feeling his heat, knowing
the slow pulse of his good heart.

FOUR TREES

Birch

Standing in the snow,
"First trees after ice," you said,
pressed your head against the bark,
wanting to hear their thaw begin.

Holly

By the door, you are planting,
peeling back turf, placing roots,
heeling in. A female: for the berries,
for the free birds, against lightning.

Ash

That last unspoken storm and in the morning
we must clear the road together; the black buds,
green skin, seed clusters now failed,
thrown in the ditch, sinking into thickened water.

Spruce

In half-light between rows,
I find a new, yellow stump;
rub my fingers over two adjacent years,
spread resin on the heartwood.

CHURCH IN SPAIN WITH TWO WOMEN

A thistle graveyard
and the sudden dark,
slow return to unswept floors,
the walls of palest blue,
plaster fallen, an outline
of oceans and continents
left behind and the roof
leaking light and dust,
onto broken glass,
San Miguel, a reflection
to the mother fully-draped
on her altar, looking down
with halo but no breasts.
She wants to forgive me again
as a spider runs
from the bird shit on her back,
settles on one brown eye.
And I imagine you here
taking flowers from the altar,
standing with the light,
your hand on my shoulder:
never done it in a church,
smiling, pulling me against you,
against the blue wall
with its map of the world.

ERRATA

The sun was rising, not setting.
What is said is always meant.
Harm should read *home*.
For coldness assume restraint.

All ambiguity is constructive.
Fiends should now be *friends*.
It was May, not March.
Ignore all negatives.

For *loathe* read *love*.
This poem was given not found.
Replace each question with an answer.
She is never mentioned.

That noise was in fact birdsong.
Erase should be *rose*.
All stray feet will return
and this rhyme never closes

as I thankfully
and finally run out
of all irony, turn off the computer,
reach for my coat.

SAFE HOUSE AT THE END OF THE LINE

a. where it will be

By the Northern Ocean, at the peninsula's tip,
unmarked on the best maps, known only to wise seals
and brightly coloured migrants blown well off course.

At the end of a road starved to a track between stationary sheep,
thinning to the once surveyed line this contour takes
along quick slopes and shears.

Squatting among trees, wind firm, water tight,
grown up from hot vents and cracks to let some fine child
mould lava; making *house*, building *home*.

b. what will be in it

Red rooms pulsing gently, a secret tunnel
in the cellar, leading to the lowlands,
known only by my friends and good relations;
my brother's unburnt guitar, resting beneath his bed;
a blonde woman drawing trees; the tall clock
my tall grandfather made when he was still tall;
the smell of something good and wholesome,
yet to be decided; a space by the window
once laughed in by my father and mother,
next to a space now laughed in by a blonde child
drawing what may be trees; the last cat
I stroked; my yellow cagoule; a variety
of favourite rocks arranged on shelves,
in chronological order from time's breakfast
to the approaching abrupt end.

CLEARING

(Loch Carron, Wester Ross)

Taking a break from all good company,
in recovery at last, I drive.
Here are white houses, accidental Zen gardens
of freshly brushed gravel and driftwood
from the loch. Here is *Doonbye*, *The Auld School*,
Brambles and *Rockview*; safely glazed against
the elemental and even worse.

The Highland Service Unit is closed.
Its ambulance rests. Free Presbyterians
stand by each corner and children
cycle diminishing circles.
I drive. A ball is kicked towards the sun,
two youths count its fall. I drive, giving way
at each passing place, wanting a store

of compassion, but no still warm pots
or tartan weave and here is a birchwood,
ruin studded, ivy and mosses
helping to forget. I drive to the end
of the road, a locked gate, foreland, beach.
Kelps rot in a neat line. A cormorant
dives and does not reappear. I choose

a perfect, flat pebble; smooth, as I recall
the skin of your neck. I draw back, crouch,
skim the stone and it bounces in the troughs
between waves, between the breaths of the sea,
turning north past Raasay and Rona
gathering speed along the Inner Sound,
away from me, towards the large ocean.

Andrew Waterhouse was born in Lincolnshire in 1958. He lives in Northumberland, where he works as a teacher and freelance writer. He received a Northern Arts Writer's Award in 1997. *In* is his first collection.

These poems travel inner and outer territories looking for a home. Shifting between the bleak and the playful; their voice is quiet, rational and ironic; their subjects are love, invertebrates, the end of the world, illness and cardigans.

YOU ARE NOT EVERYBODY'S CUP OF TEA

A catalogue copy of this book is available in the British Library.

Unless otherwise noted, the author and the publisher make no explicit guarantees as the accuracy of the information contained in this book may differ based on individual experiences and context.

For enquires, email:
hello@elohoefemuai.co.uk

http://www.elohoefemuai.co.uk

978-1-5272-6661-2

Dedication

This book is dedicated to my husband U.J Efemuai, thank you for believing in me, for standing by me, for being patient with me and for supporting me every step of the way.

Acknowledgement

Grateful to God for the giftings and talents as well as the privilege and opportunity to serve.

To my kids Nathan, Aimee and Josh thank you for loving me the way you do.

To everyone who has helped birth this vision in one way or the other, my coaches, cheerleaders, Arise with Eloho and Heartsong Live Family. I really do appreciate your support. Special thanks to my launch team thank you to every single one of you for being my dream boosters.

What people are saying about 'You Are Not Everybody's Cup of Tea'.

Reading through "You are not everyone's cup of tea" is like having a heart to heart talk with the author. The read is easy, the flow is smooth and conversational. And for anyone who knows Eloho, you can practically feel her having a chummy conversation with you. Eloho bares it all holding back nothing, sharing her experiences with her audience. If you have ever gone through rejection, low self-esteem and a struggle for approval from others then this book is for you. On the other hand, if you have been lucky not to have had those experiences this book can serve as a reference point to help others. I must say that as I read the book I had quite a few aha moments as much of what Eloho shared resonated with me. From the deep reserves of her life's experiences Eloho is fulfilling her passion to inspire. This book from my point of view should be in every home and on everyone's library shelf. It will definitely bless all who read it.

Erumena Amata author The Dimpsey Chronicles, Lagos Nigeria

Eloho's book is one of those easy reads that will leave the reader with a lasting impact. The saying people like those that are Real more than those that are Right is what this book epitomizes. It is based on Eloho's reality and will challenge every reader to revisit their reality and how that can be the anchor holding them back. It’s definitely one to read and read again. *Stephen Ojo-Financial City Trader*

In a world where people hardly speak of progress, Eloho has unashamedly put her journey into this beautiful piece. She shared practical steps on how she arrived at the authentic and bold life that she enjoys today. Although some of the experiences cost her so much pain at the time, she has allowed herself experience healing and she is determined to help others find healing and wholeness. I highly recommend this book to anyone who is struggling with low esteem and approval addiction. This book is a liberating tool and it should be on every bookshelf.

Ola Olaleye Authenticity Coach, CEO The Esther's Company

Your style of book is very conversational. Whilst reading it I felt that you were there in the room with me. Your voice came alive on the pages. I love your simple, no nonsense, clear and authentic style which makes it an instant page turner. I love the way you explore your dreams - test your dreams and make adaptation for current situation you find you self in. I had a light bulb moment through reading this book in that I have to work daily on myself and not just practically but first and foremost mentally. Thought out the book - I loved the way you questioned your own faith and belief. By telling your story in a very simple way - I found that I could relate to it without being theoretical. It's a very emotionally, hard hitting account of your journey with tips and advice. The story is well crafted and allows your insight into Eloho and exposes her vulnerability; in doing so the truth has set her on the path to inner freedom. *Annette West Network Marketer Edinburgh*

Very inspirational and thought of book. Good flow...Congratulations!!

- *UJ Efemuai- Snr Project Engineer*

Just to say thank you for buying my book, I am offering you a free 30 mins discovery session with me. Click link below let's connect.

http://elohoefemuai.co.uk/discovery-session/

Book Description

I used to think that my self-worth depended on what others thought or said about me and for years I struggled to fit in. I thought that I had to be everybody's "cup of tea". This not only crippled my personal growth and self-development, but it also affected my relationships. I realized I was going around the same circle over and over again, making the same mistakes and I genuinely felt that I had a problem. I tried to grow myself but struggled until I realized that to grow myself, I had to know myself and see worth in myself.

I have come to realize that one thing that cripples the growth and progress of many of us is not necessarily an external factor, such as other people's opinions, as we often imagine; rather, it is you and I being the antagonists of our very own story.

At every stage of our lives, you will agree with me that certain factors that should have amplified your growth are the same factors you have allowed to tear you down. I hope that through the pages of this book, I would be able to inspire you to overcome these challenges, using these factors to your advantage, to set your success journey in motion as I have; through understanding and acceptance of your identity.

The truth is that identity is everything to a person. We cannot grow ourselves if we do not know and understand ourselves. You must understand yourself, identify your strengths, weaknesses, your uniqueness and use them to your advantage. In this book, I share with you my story of personal growth, self-development and issues such as

- Lack of self-confidence
- Self-worth
- Impostor syndrome, and
- Authenticity

Table of Contents

Introduction

Self-development, self-growth, self-confidence are issues many people continually deal with. This is mostly a problem for many of us because, as the name implies, it should be about the "self," that is, you. The things you perceive should be great for you, but instead, we often generate our worth, self-value, and confidence based on what others think of us.

For years I struggled with a lack of confidence and low self-esteem; I never felt good enough. I always found myself moving in the direction that did not reflect how I valued myself and I struggled to fit in. I always felt like I needed to please everyone so they could like me, but rather than be liked, I was hurt terribly. In those years, I forgot about a very critical factor in the entire equation: I forgot about myself. Maybe I did not forget, but I neglected myself and based the value of myself on the opinions and ideas of others.

However, although it took me years to understand all I will be sharing in this book. I have decided that no woman, in fact, nobody irrespective of gender, should be forced to settle for a particular quality of living that is not pleasing on so many levels based on the opinions of people and their perception of things.

I finally began to see the worth in myself after several years; today I have evolved. I am no longer that girl, and I love me for me, I am good enough. Despite my mistakes, my weaknesses and insecurities I am good enough and I am now coaching other women who have struggled with that feeling of never being good enough on how to stop doubting their greatness, overcome that feeling of lack and step in to be the women they were created to be.

My desire and passion is to help everyone who has battled with a lack of confidence and low self-esteem break free from the stereotypes to become the person they were designed to be. I do this by teaching people the tools that helped me overcome my insecurities to start a ministry and grow a business. I also show them how they can show up consistently on social media to generate leads for their business. I help them with strategies that help increase their visibility and give voice to their business, brand product and ministry on social media.

This book has been written from my personal experience, and I hope that as you read through its pages, you will be able to relate with my story and take my challenges and victories to help you solve your own challenges and create your victories. My hope is that you will not feel alone and allow me to be with you every step of the way.

CHAPTER ONE

Know Your Worth

The level of worth you attach to yourself directly translates to your level of self-esteem and confidence. Although low self-esteem is not something a lot of people aspire to develop, many people find themselves experiencing deep levels of low self-esteem throughout their years. This thought or idea may have been instigated by past experiences or opinions of others about you that have been adapted to become your perspective of yourself. Generally speaking, your self-esteem is your perspective or opinion of yourself; it is the value and worth you have consciously attached to your person through the years. It is from your level of self-esteem that every other growth begins.

That being said, instead of this factor to be developed based on deep understanding and enlightenment of yourself by yourself, many of us are distracted by external influences, which could be anything, ranging from family, peer influence, social media, and even entertainment.

Your self-esteem is primarily determined by whatever you have consciously or subconsciously hinted to your mind to be the perfect image. These hints are selected throughout the day, in different situations, whether you gave that idea little or no thought.

Have you ever felt out of place because you felt like you did not measure up? Have you ever felt because you were different, nobody understood you? Or have you ever compared yourself to others and felt empty or not worth it? I have. This happens in the subtlest situations where many people have experienced this feeling, whether you would agree or not. Most of us have been in situations where we thought we were less important or did not matter compared to others because we did not do things like them or even look the part. Well, if you are one of the few that would own up, you are not alone.

How to Increase Your Self-Esteem

I know I have experienced a fraction of this; low self-esteem, which made me question my worth and importance for some time. One of the things that I struggled with was my physical appearance. As a teenager growing up, I was taller and skinnier than most of the girls my age, and I always felt out of place. I got teased a lot for being so tall and skinny, and that affected my self-esteem such that it got to a point where I could not walk straight up. Slouching became my routine. I had bad posture - I would always have my shoulders down and my mother would always encourage me to walk up straight. At a point, I could not even walk properly because I was so timid. Also, I started to take all sorts so I could gain some weight.

Your self-esteem not only affects your psychological consciousness or opinion of yourself, but it also takes its toll on your appearance. I was timid, and if I was walking down a road and saw a group of people together, I always felt they were talking about me and my height. I was extremely self-conscious of my height, which is obviously a good one but it was not in my case. My height bothered me for a very long time. I thought I was not good enough because I wasn't like others.

Often, it is not the case that you are not worth anything. Instead, you undervalue yourself and neglect your potential because you have been riddled by low self-esteem for a long time. For me it was my height. For you it may be something else that has made you undervalue yourself. When people are asked about their worth, specific questions like, "What are you worth?" "How valuable do you think you are?" They respond with generic answers such as "I am highly valuable" or "A lot."

Nevertheless, you should be confident and give more of yourself because you are worth more than you believe in every situation. You should never settle for the general opinions of value that people have attached to your role in their life. Instead, thrive on understanding yourself, discovering yourself, and building a perspective of yourself independent of the opinions others have about you. Good self-esteem is not restricted to a particular category of people, no one is born perfect, and no one grows to be perfect. However, you can strive towards a lifestyle of perfection with the following tips for building better self-esteem.

- Redefine the term "self-esteem". For some people, the problem stems from an inadequate or improper understanding of the concept. They think self-esteem has everything to do with their appearance and not the mind, so they do all in their power to create some changes to their outward looks, getting little or no results. On the contrary, if you are on the road to building your self-esteem, you must understand that it is more psychological than physical. Everything begins in the mind. Your self-worth should not be dependent on how you look. This does not mean that if you feel like you need to hit the gym, or do a makeover, you should not. You can, but do not do this with the mindset that this would start a massive change in your self-development. Your self-esteem should not be based solely on your appearance. You should also focus on your morals, intelligence, interaction, belief system, and mindset. Confidence does not start from your skin and sink into your heart; instead, it begins from within and shines through in all your dealings.

- Set Goals: would you like to build a successful business, brand, career or ministry? Set goals! Do you want to have excellent grades? Set goals! Do you want to be the best version of yourself? Set goals! There is no restriction on what you can set goals for. The list is endless. It helps you to stretch yourself beyond your own perceived capabilities. Therefore, building your self-esteem is building mental muscles, and like any physical goal to build muscles, it will demand focus, time, and dedication. The best way to ensure that you remain on track is by setting specific goals through your journey. While this may be true, it is not enough to simply set goals. You must take action and when you meet a particular target, acknowledge and celebrate your wins, even the smallest wins you have. I choose to celebrate every little win and victory. Be your own cheerleader because your entire journey is dependent on your opinion of yourself, and if you are unable to celebrate yourself, you will subconsciously seek validation from others. This does not mean that you should not respect the opinion of others; rather, ensure that you are able to filter through these opinions. Identify those that are targeted towards building you up and others that may tear you down.

- Love your current self. Instead of detesting your present person that is continuously searching for approval and validation, embrace her and love her. Love yourself and push yourself till you achieve that specific goal you desire. Repeat to yourself those things that you have been structured to hate about yourself, embrace them, and understand that they are what makes you unique. Remember, I used to be so bothered about my height, now it has become one of the things I love the most about myself.

Nowadays, I laugh at the thought that my height was the very source of my low self-esteem. At that point, however, it was not funny. I felt out of place and did not feel good enough. Isn't it amazing how we allow what we consider inadequacies to affect us? Consider this: People wear heels to look the part, and there I was with my natural God-given height which I never appreciated because some people made fun of me. People's words can make or break you. Thankfully even though those words had the potential to break me, they did not. Today I still get teased by people about my height, but because I have chosen to love and celebrate myself for who I am, it does not bother me anymore. Now I am comfortable in my own skin. I fell in love with my height and decided I was going to celebrate my uniqueness. People have wondered about my love for photos. There was a time I did not like seeing myself in pictures, but when I started to accept me for me, I decided that I was going to make a bold statement by taking photos and declaring "this is me, this is how I look, this is how I am. I love it, I love myself, and I am beautiful just the way I am, and I would not wish to be anybody else." When people would ask me, “Why do you like taking photos a lot?” I just smile and let them keep wondering but it is my own way of making a bold statement to say; “Hey I am beautiful, I am valued, I am a person of worth, I love myself, and if I am not your cup of tea, I can be somebody else's cup of coffee or hot chocolate."

For you, it may not be your height; it might be something else. You may feel like you are not talented enough or the right person for that job or even that you are not an expert, but would you believe me if I told you that you are good enough and that you are exactly what you need? You have what it takes to succeed. You are unique and in all the world there can never be another you. Insecurities, inadequacies, and all, you have a lot to offer the world. You have got to accept you for you. It is not enough for people to tell you how great you are or how beautiful you are. If you do not see yourself as great or beautiful, a thousand hearts on Instagram or a thousand likes on Facebook would never be enough. Believe in yourself. Believe in the woman or the man that you were created to be.

CHAPTER TWO

Battling Rejection, Unforgiveness and Undervaluing Your Potential

---

Many times, our need to copy others or be like others stems from the need to receive approval. Be that as it may, a lot of us fail to consider the problem while we chase this because we have somewhat put ourselves in harm's way based on our desires. We have put the responsibility of guidance and protection of our lives on someone else while it should be our singular most crucial responsibility to ourselves.

Therefore, we should not be surprised when we find people taking advantage of us. You know why? We have unwittingly given them the power to have so much control. If you happen to have fallen into this situation, what then is your next step?

What do you do when someone that should protect you takes advantage of you and abuses you? You would agree with me that someone you have trusted taking this trust for granted is one of the most devastating things that could happen to anyone.

I was taken for granted, and that abuse affected me so much for a long time. The hold it had on me was firm and more than I could have imagined. Because of it, I felt unworthy, guilty, and I was continually condemning myself. I felt empty and that everyone could see through me. It affected my trust in future relationships, and I felt like I always had to cover up, which even affected my marriage. This was something I had to contend with for years.

On the outside, it looked like I had it all together and that everything was okay, but it was not. I was dealing with a lot on the inside of me. At some point my husband had to step in and would always say to me, "Let your past go, do you want to affect your future and present because of your past?". But I could not. As much as I tried my past was weighing me down. It had such a hold over me.

How to Exist Beyond the Shadows of Past Self

Eventually, during my journey, I came to the conclusion that I had to grow, move past everything that I had experienced, and allow the past to remain where it belonged. Although this idea seemed easy on paper, it was not as easy when it came to practice. To ensure that the past remained in the past and to create a future that would not be tainted by my past, I had to be conscious of some specific changes.

Firstly, I had to recognize the value within me and stop seeking approval from others. As a woman of faith, I had to go back to my Creator's manual to find out what exactly He thought about me and how

He sees me. I began to meditate and focus on how He sees me, and how He made me the way I am for a purpose.

As a result of the abuse I had experienced, I felt empty, invisible. It was like if you had some supernatural power and could see into my soul, you would only find a massive void within, and I was determined to prove this thought wrong. I felt like this was what everyone thought of me, I was nothing, so I was bent on being something or everything to everybody. This made me to always seek approval from everyone, and I needed people to make me feel like I was essential to them. I wanted to be someone, to exist for other people but not necessarily myself.

There was a strong need to please others irrespective of the things it would do to me. I did not value myself at all, or even recognize my own worth. At this point, I believe it is possible to say, I felt my recognition was dependent on the approval of others and the group of people that thought I was important. I did not see worth in myself, and so I felt that I always had to beg for approval. I was such an approval addict that if I didn't get the approval I desired, I thought I had done something wrong or had not measured up. I needed people to like me, so I had to always go out of my way to please people or be there for them even when it was not convenient for me. In the process, I made a lot of mistakes, hurting the closest people to me and was even hugely misunderstood.

Do you know how you can sometimes feel like if you do certain things for people, they will like you more? That was precisely what was happening to me at this stage, but I did not get my expected result. You would think that the more approval I got, the better I would feel, but this was not the case at all; the more I tried, the more emptiness I felt. Instead of empowering me, this idea kept draining me, but I am thankful for my faith that sustained me.

Something else thing that helped me overcome this phase of my life was speaking up. One of such times, when I was berating myself and feeling like a failure, I spoke to a dear friend in tears and she said, Eloho you need counselling. Although I am a trained counsellor, I will refer you to someone who can help. Sometimes, we tend to overlook the importance of listeners, befrienders, counselors or therapists in our lives. They are of huge assistance to anyone willing to appreciate themselves independently and see beyond their past experiences. This is why I have now chosen to be a befriender to others. I have recently just completed a training on developing my listening skills so that I can be there for others. As they say you cannot give what you do not have, you cannot take people to a place you have not been.

Speaking about the abuse and every other thing I was feeling helped me, the first 3 sessions were full of tears, but it set me on a new path by setting me free.

I had been holding on so much to my past and all I went through, and it was affecting my marriage. I could not be completely free or open with my husband, needless to say he was frustrated. I held in so much, and it affected me in so many ways, but I wanted to be able to be free with my him and not have to hold back anything which is one of the reasons I decided to speak up. Speaking about the things I was going through helped me see that anything that happened to me was not my fault.

I had to forgive myself and tell myself it was not my fault. I had to be intentional about letting go of everything that had a hold on me. In the past, several times, my husband would say, "The past is gone, leave it alone." But funny enough who would have thought I would be the one preaching it to people, talking to people and saying, “You know what, you cannot change the past, but you can at least leave it alone”. I could not let go of my past at first; it was difficult because I was keeping so much in.

Although I understand that talking about your experiences can be difficult, it is more helpful to discuss it than hold it in. It was not an easy process, but I am free now, which is the most important thing I am thankful for the journey so far, I am not there yet, I am a work in progress, but things are much better now. I am not where I used to be. Now, I am able to help others who are being held back from living a confident and fulfilled life because of one thing or the other. I always say now that although you had no control over the past and cannot change it, the future can be determined by the choices you make today. What you do today matters.

The past is gone, and we can leave it alone. You can forgive that person who hurt you, that person who told you, you were not good enough, that person or people who mocked you, that person who betrayed you, that person who lied to you, that person who abused you and took advantage of you and even that person who told you, you will amount to nothing no matter how you try. Forgiveness is a process that does not happen overnight, but if you are willing, you can be completely healed. I had to forgive myself and even forgive everyone who hurt me. Forgiveness of the past is a massive part of your progress. It helped me and it can help you too.

Another thing that helped me at this stage of my life was reading. The content we take in is one of the things that we generally have little regard for in the world. We are what we read. Usually, the role of the information we allow into our minds is given little concern in determining our state of mind and reality, and this is a substantial contributing factor. Reading the right things was able to heal me to a large extent.

I reached a point on my growth journey when I realized that everything begins in the mind, "as a man thinks so is he". You are your thoughts.

One of the books I read that helped me was "As A Man Thinketh" by James Allen. It was part of a coaching program I was on. Although a very small book, it completely transformed my mindset. One of the things that it did for me then was that it made me understand that although we cannot change the things that happen around us, we can choose how we respond to them. It was a surprise and a wakeup call for me when I read that book, genuinely enlightening. The book talks about the mind being a garden and how, when you are growing your garden, you do not allow weeds to grow in it. You tend your garden, and you take care of it. Likewise, our minds are like gardens and the negative thoughts that come into it are like weeds, so you have to intentionally and consciously weed your mind of those negative thoughts.

All those years, all I had been doing was focusing on the wrong thoughts, focusing on the wrong things, allowing the weeds to take over my garden. So somebody says something, and I begin to meditate on that, someone says something else about me, does something to me and I would always feel it was my fault, and I was to blame. I was allowing the weeds to take root in my garden, chasing out the flowers that were already planted. At a point, if someone says to me "we need to talk" I always felt something was wrong, I remember a dear friend said to me once "I do not want you to think every time I say let us talk it is something negative". That is how much I allowed weeds take root in the garden of my mind.

But thankfully, reading this book alongside my Bible helped me a lot. Believe me everything does really begin from the mind. What are you allowing into your mind, what are you believing about yourself? I studied my Bible to find out more about the things that God had said about me. I went looking for the scriptures that talked about my value, my importance to God, how special I am to Him and His deep love for me. I began to do that consciously and consistently, to renew my mind, to clear it and say, "Yes, people can say things about me, and it is okay. They can do things to me, and it is still okay because what God thinks about me and how

I see myself is the most important thing". I realized that although I cannot change what has happened, I have a choice to control how I respond to it.

I started to learn how to respond, not react. In the past, I would react, if someone had done something or said something to me, I would get agitated and start crying. I would either begin to tell people about it or go into my shell, and if I say something to someone, the person tells another person and the cycle of telling other people continues. But I started to learn to respond and not to react, which has helped me a lot on my journey which is why I am now helping others with the tools that helped me. You do not have to please everyone. You cannot be everyone's "cup of tea".

Everyone does not have to like you. Funny how I am telling you this when I was all about the same thing at some point in my life, but the earlier you realize this, the better.

When I first started my business, I priced myself so low because I felt I was not worth the price other people were charging. I felt I did not have what it took. Yes, I know people would say but there is an entry point. While I agree with that, I would also like to state that how you do anything is how you do everything. I realized this need to please everyone had somehow found its way into my business and after a while I said I was not having it and so I changed my prices to reflect my worth. Recently someone asked me my price and said it was too expensive and I said that was ok. If it was in time past because I needed to be liked, I would have sold myself short even though it would not have reflected my worth.

Not everyone will get you but that is ok. Not everyone will be able to afford your prices and that is ok as well. Never sell yourself short. When I started to accept this, I became free, I was liberated and began to accept myself for myself. I started to express gratitude for everything around me. I began to tell myself I was enough. What I did not have, I did not need. I boldly declare that I am enough; everything that I need is in me and within me. I decided to raise my value and realized that I did not need any fixing; I did not need anybody to fix me. I heard words like “you need to," “you need to go, you need to do" But I realized that I did not need fixing. I was alright, and I was complete. I just needed to grow myself and increase my own value. How you see yourself is how everyone sees you. All the time, I was giving off the wrong energy.

Straight off, I would like to encourage you with this: never live to please others because nothing beneficial can come from it. You are feeding their cause, their vision, their goals, who do you think would be made happy? Them, of course, because it is their life that is being improved, and you are feeding their energy by draining yourself because you are not feeding your body with that nutrient that makes you content. Your nutrient could be anything; it could be the smallest things like wearing a specific dress simply because you like it and not based on the opinion of others. Therefore, your value can only be found when you search deep within yourself, not when you search deeply in the vision of others.

CHAPTER THREE

Impostor Syndrome: Help I Am A Fraud

Many people thought I was fine when I had issues dealing with self- acceptance, validation, forgiveness, and rejection. It was not evident that I had battles, which made the entire issue of self-development somewhat difficult because I was hiding.

On the outside, I looked like this really strong person, you know. I had been organizing concerts for years, and so I looked like this amazon of a woman to everyone but myself. Most people must have been convinced that I certainly had it all together, but inside of me, I was battling with so much, dealing with so many things.

My relationship with myself that is, my subconscious was not great, I was in an internal battle with myself, work was not good because my lack of self-confidence was always affecting me and even my marital life was not spared. My marriage was in big trouble because of everything I was battling with. There were communication and connection issues; I was not free to be myself because I felt the constant need to keep some aspect of my life hidden. I could not freely express myself, and I tried, and tried hard; but something was holding me back from being the woman that I was created to be. So, I struggled. However, there was no external force holding me back; I was my anchor, my barricade. My constant need for validation and fear of rejection prevented me from achieving the level of greatness I was capable of attaining. All this happened because I had low self-esteem.

The Right Company

At work, I did not fit in, or at least that is how I felt. To me, I did not belong, so at work, I avoided having any relations of any kind with other people. I was unable to utter a single word to anyone. I would put on my headphones and listen to my music because I felt that my opinion did not matter. I convinced myself that people would and could not understand me; there was nothing I could say to change their perspective of anything I had to say, so it was better I kept to myself. Can you imagine what we do to ourselves?

We would have meetings where I had things to say, but I was usually too scared to mention anything. I thought that they would not like me or they would not like what I had to say or that they would shut me down and so I just kept it all to myself and kept it in so I would go to work and go home with little or no communication through the day.

However, even in that low self-esteem stage, there was someone who was kind to me and made me feel comfortable with her. There is always someone ready to be your friend. Usually, there could be more than one person willing to understand your experiences. Whenever I was with her, I was a completely different person. It is crucial that you are conscious of the people you are surrounded with; the right company can either help build your self-esteem or break whatever you have managed to develop in the first place.

This particular category of people who are willing to assist you in your journey to self-confidence and validation do not always have to be your friends, colleagues, or family members. Some of them could be mentors, service providers, or even coaches. However, it is left to you to accept these people so that they can provide further help. You must understand that if a particular individual is of no advantage to you, then it is advisable that you grow, excluding that person's presence from your life.

One of such people I would describe as the right company is my coach. I can never forget the first thing my coach said to me, "You are an eagle, but you are trying to fly with chickens." I was confused when I first heard that, but the bottom line was the fact that I did not place any value on myself and refused to recognize my worth, so I allowed any and everybody into my space. The problem with this was that they could not give me the approval that I needed; they could not give me what I desired because only my Creator can give me that approval.

I know it takes a while and it is a process, but if you choose to grow yourself and surround yourself with people who see the gold in you and bring out the best in you, you will experience a new you. I mean, if you had told me that I would be writing a book a few years ago and encouraging people with my story, I would have said no way. But now because I have experienced it, I am able to encourage someone else, I am able to inspire other people to realize that you do not have to live on that street.

You may have been abused like I was, you may have been rejected, and physically kicked out of a place that was like your comfort zone, but you can still be the person that you were created to be and change your address. You can still do the things that you have always wanted to do. You are free of any condemnation or guilt. Yes, you may have made mistakes, but your mistakes do not define you. I had to get to that point where I looked at my mistakes eyeball to eyeball and declared, "yes, I did it, and I am sorry that I made those mistakes, but that is not who I am". I continually had to tell myself that I am not that person. I do not live there anymore. I remember telling someone when they brought up my past, that this girl no longer lives at that address. I had to let it sink into my consciousness that I was special. I mean growing up I knew that I was special, I knew that there was something special about me, but because I had suffered all of these things, I was not sure who I was anymore. I lost my identity.

So, I want to say to you, do not try to win the approval of others at all costs. Just be yourself, and be confident in your skin, love yourself for yourself and for who you are; recognize your value, accept it and believe it, focus on your assignment, know yourself and grow yourself. Above all, surround yourself with the people who inspire and encourage you. When you are around people who celebrate you, people who see the worth in you, you excel, and you shine brighter.

DEALING WITH IMPOSTOR SYNDROME

Wikipedia describes **impostor syndrome** as a psychological pattern in which one doubts one's accomplishments and has a persistent internalized fear of being exposed as a "fraud."

If you have ever felt any of these, then you probably struggle with imposter syndrome.

"I am not expert enough to be able to do this"

"No one is going to bother reading my posts or watch my live stream"

"I am not good enough. My music does not sound like so and so."

"Who would read my book".

"Somebody else is already doing this, what difference would it make".

Although some people might think of me as strong, confident and an expert now, this was not always the case. I suffered from impostor syndrome. I battled with accepting my success and level of expertise. I thought I was a fraud and was not worthy of the attention and audience I had. I even questioned my authority to assist other people, but I realized that this was caused by a lack of confidence, self-worth, and low self-esteem.

Sometime in my life, where confidence and validation were significant issues in my life, I suffered rejection from a body where I felt safe, and that just further affected me. Imagine that the very roof that was protecting you from the rain, all crumbling down one day without any warning, destroying the entire house that is meant to be your shelter. I was devastated by this, it compounded the problem, and I further did not see any worth or value in myself. I am a singer, and I know I have a good voice, but because I was suffering from that low self-esteem and identity crisis, I could not express myself well when I sang. I would organize my concerts but not be bold enough to sing more than one song because I was scared. I was scared that people would find out that I was not that good. I feared for my success.

At some point, I began to feel like I had a problem. I had seen a particular trend in my relationships, and I was trying so hard to win people's approval or get them on my side. As I said earlier, that did not work out. I had to get to the point where I had to consciously and intentionally place value on myself. Therefore, in this journey of building self- confidence, and self-worth, you are only as successful as you are intentional.

It took years before I was able to finally step up and be bold enough to do the things I was created to do.

These are the things I did that helped me overcome impostor syndrome

- I chose to accept myself for me and express gratitude for everything around me. After all God made me this way and everything He does is perfect.
- I stopped the comparison game and started believing in my own worth.
- I realized that I did not need fixing; I just needed to realize my own value.
- I read books that helped me and surrounded myself with people who inspired and encouraged me.
- I realized that I could not be everybody's cup of tea, but I

could be someone's cup of coffee or hot chocolate.

- I focused on being a blessing to someone and stopped seeking for approval. I focused on my assignment.
- I practiced affirmations,

I still use my daily affirmations by the way. Oh, my goodness, you should see my notes and journals! Every opportunity I get, especially when those negative thoughts start coming and I start to feel I am not good enough I begin to use my affirmations and declare to myself, "I am good enough, I am worth it, I am valued, I am enough, I believe in myself, I believe in my ability to succeed." These daily affirmations still help me on my growth journey.

CHAPTER FOUR

What Is the Concept of "Authenticity"?

The concept of authenticity is not something many of us are familiar with, and it is not even a concept that we hear every day. However, it is a concept that is unavoidably connected to our happiness. To be authentic directly means that you are comfortable and relaxed in your identity. It is the idea that allows you to let go of your regular thought of perfection and accept that whatever you are is the actual definition of perfection, and this is done without undermining anyone.

Lack of authenticity can be a problem in many situations. When I first started my business, I thought I had to keep my business separate from who I am and I was trying so hard, but I was not attracting my ideal clients. By day I was this powerful gospel artistes and woman of faith inspiring people on the radio but for some strange reason I felt I did not have to show that side of me in my business. I tell you, it was a struggle as I was not being my true authentic self. Eventually I came to the point where I had to accept all of me and show up as me in every area of my life. Now I am beginning to attract my ideal clients in my business.

For you to be authentic in all situations, you must be willing to accept yourself and show up as yourself regardless of what others think or say; you must be able to do everything I have spoken about in previous chapters - abandon your need for external validation, forgive yourself and others, recognize the talent, and potentials that exist in you.

I remember when I first started radio broadcasting and felt like I had to put on a "radio voice", I felt I needed to speak in a certain way until my radio mentor said to me "you know you don't have to put on a radio voice, just be yourself, speak the exact same way you would naturally speak when you are having a conversation". Bottom line be your authentic self. Be you and do you.

Something that I have learned from my experiences through the years is the fact that there is no particular way to experience joy, peace, gratitude and satisfaction unless you are able to accept your uniqueness and appreciate yourself.

After I released my first album, I heard things like "Your voice is not like *so and so,"* someone in particular said to me *"So and So person would have done this song better"*. I was told that my voice was not good enough and was compared to a lot of other people.

Although I was strong enough to overlook their comments, it hurt me and I was determined to be me and do me. I was determined to show up as me, trusting that someone out there would appreciate my music and so I chose to promote my album. My determination notwithstanding, I did not realize there was still a lot of unbelief in myself. Then boom! Impostor Syndrome came to show its face again. I was dealing with the feeling of fraud at the same time I was trying to sell my uniqueness. I was so uncertain of my talent on a lot of levels. I thought I could not express myself for fear of what people would say. I wanted to receive feedback. In fact, I needed it to grow, to be better to some extent, but I feared that they would not like it. Would they even listen to it, listen to me? Would they consider it good enough? I may not be Whitney Houston, I sure do not sound like her, but I have a voice. My voice is beautiful, it is gracious, and I love it.

My voice is perfectly and uniquely mine. I know it now, and I am proud of it. Now, I have reached that stage where I have become free to express myself.

HOW TO EMBRACE YOUR AUTHENTICITY

Your authentic self is everything that makes you stand out from the next person; it is your peculiarity. Many times, you might find people in your life that may try to pass this off as you being too opinionated, weird, different, but trust me, this is not always a bad thing. Your uniqueness is that one fact or thing that makes you different when compared to others. Next time, you are around people trying to make you feel like an outcast or people that call you weird, embrace this, and see the good side of this comment. There are always two sides to a coin, the head and tail; so why we always choose to see the bad side of things? It sure does baffle me. If you have found it difficult to embrace your authentic or uniqueness, the following are some tips to help you.

- Let go of the need for perfectionism instead strive for excellence. Focus on doing your best and let go of trying to be perfect
- This one is my favorite. Do it now and perfect it later. Do it afraid.
- Celebrate the wonderful person that you are, your uniqueness and imperfections. Someone once said we are perfectly imperfect.

- Stop seeking validation from others because they would certainly see you as different. Therefore, before you put yourself in a situation where people are constantly dropping ideas or comments about you, ensure that you have properly understood yourself.
- Take time to identify and accept your uniqueness. One thing that you have to understand on this journey is that you cannot be in a haste to embracing acceptance. You have to allow yourself the time to wholly and carefully unfold. Not some halfway development that did not even unfold naturally. Allow yourself

the time and dedicate yourself to achieving the needed development.

- Authenticity does not only concern your talent or your personality. It can be narrowed to your opinions and viewpoints of situations. Develop your knowledge and understanding on various subjects, so that you can create ideas and opinions that work well for you and not opinions that are agreed upon for the sole reason of pleasing others.
- Acknowledge **ALL** comments. The funny thing was I did not get only negative comments. There were many other positive comments, but I chose to focus on

the not so good ones. This is what many of us do to ourselves. Most of the time, a lot of people appreciate us, giving us positive feedback, positive remarks, and many other positive acknowledgments. Still, for some reason, we always choose to identify with the negative. I mean, why would you not rather choose to focus on the few that accept and celebrate you. It is a choice. I do not know why we do it, but we always choose to focus on the comments that are not healthy, that are not positive, and all of this affected my confidence greatly. The comments and opinions of others about us are only effective to the extent that we allow them to be.

Because I have embraced my authentic self, now when I get comments like, "you do not sound like so and so person" or "so and so person would have done this song better than you did it," it does not bother me. Before now, comments like that would crush me, and I would start to reconsider my reason for starting such a journey in the first place

Every one of us has an authentic self. Nevertheless, it is left for you to accept it and own it.

CHAPTER FIVE

Stepping Out of Your Comfort Zone

Imagine a life where you can travel to all your favourite places, whenever you want. A life where you were not so concerned about the opinions of others, in which you held yourself in high esteem. A life where you get whatever you want, whenever you want it because you were bold enough to go after it. Such a life would be glorious wouldn't it? Sadly, the world does not work that way naturally. It only happens when we are ready to put in the work to acquire that which we desire. We exist in a world where we have to put in our all to achieve success, and a world where we cannot just do whatever we want, whenever we want. In a nutshell, we live in a world filled with responsibilities we have to uphold, responsibilities that are dependent on understanding our individual characters and identities.

All of these imaginations that you often have, are what I like to call, your comfort zone. This zone is characterized by the idea of never wanting to go through any difficulties or discomfort but still getting all you want from life. Well, as much as we want that to happen, it cannot. You have to find a way to extract yourself from this zone. Otherwise, it will slowly eat away at your life until you look back and all you see is a sea of regrets. On the news or social media, you get to see so many successful people and their success stories. Every time you come across it you think to yourself, "I want this and many more." Well, you cannot get 'this and many more' if you keep sitting firmly in your comfort zone. No one ever gets successful that way. Truly, there is nothing wrong with being in your comfort zone, but it requires moderation.

To guide you through the path of stepping out of your comfort zone, I have come up with some steps you need to take to gain mastery over your comfort zone:

- Embrace Uncertainty: Humans have this funny habit of wanting to control everything. The sad truth is that we cannot control everything that happens in our lives. What we can control is our reaction to those happenings. I am sure this must sound cliché but you have to admit that it is the fact. The sooner you get over this habit of the excessive need to control everything, the easier it gets for you to get out of your comfort zone and into a successful life.

- You have to admit that one of the major reasons why most people find it hard to get out of their comfort zone is because of their drowning in a pool of 'what ifs.' "What if I try this and I am not good enough?" "What if I try out for this competition and I end up looking like a fool and embarrassing myself?" All those doubtful questions start with 'what if.' There is no problem with 'what if' questions, but why don't you try shifting them from negative to positive questions. For example, "What if I try out for this competition and I eventually win? There is no harm in trying." "What if I pitch this idea to my boss and he eventually likes it?"

- Nothing is certain, not even today. Understanding this would push you to do the seemingly scary things you have always wanted to do. Once you embrace uncertainty, no issue looks so big anymore because you have the right attitude to face it head on. Stepping out of your comfort zone from time to time also becomes easier for you. So, focus on the things you can control. When you do that, you discover that the things you can control sometimes, either wholly or partly, make up for the ones that you cannot control.

- Be willing and unwilling: The first question you should ask yourself is, “Am I willing to turn my life around?” Many of you might see this as a stupid question because you might think, “Who would not want to turn their life around?” Well, I would like to let you know that wanting something and working towards getting what you want are two completely different things. Sometimes asking yourself if you are willing, is not enough. Instead, you need to ask yourself, “Am I unwilling?” Are you unwilling to let your life remain the same? Are you unwilling to keep running away from challenges that can develop you? Asking these inverse questions go a long way in motivating you to actualize the change you want to see in your life.

- However, you must understand that not everyone is the same. For some, trying these techniques will work, and for some others it will not work. If you are in this latter category, you might find out that you may muster the willingness to change your life but not long enough to change anything. That is where the problem lies. At this stage, you must accept that you are unwilling to fundamentally change your life. Right now, in your mind you might be on the defensive saying, "That is not true. Why wouldn't I want to change my life?" Well, if you wanted to change your life so bad, why are you still sitting comfortably in your comfort zone?

- Sometimes, accepting this fact is the first step in waking yourself up to make those desired changes in your life.

- Separate Your Thoughts from Your Actions: many people believe that our thoughts automatically determine our actions; that is not true. I am sure you must have experienced situations where you are thinking one thing, but you find yourself doing the opposite of what you thought. You must have faced many instances where all you want to do is stay in bed all day, but you still find yourself getting up from that bed to finish a project or go to work. The misconception that our thoughts are necessarily equivalent to actions have caused some people to drown in their comfort zone. Throw out that line of reasoning today because it would help you take those steps that would help you leave your comfort zone when needed.

- Sometimes all you need to do to successfully leave your comfort zone is to do, instead of dwelling too much on your thoughts. Our thoughts have a way of making things look bigger than they actually are. I am big on taking action.
- Expect Everything and Accept Everything: when you eventually leave your comfort zone, do not let the addiction of expectation rule you. Fine, you have been successful in leaving your comfort zone by participating in that competition. You passed the first

round successfully. Now, you are in the next stage of the competition. At this point, you then take a look at your fellow competitors and how good they are. That seed of doubt starts to grow because what you were expecting is far different from what you are experiencing. You then start to back out of the competition because you suddenly feel like you are not good enough. Now what happened in this scenario is that you probably expected to win that competition without any challenges because you felt your idea was the best ever. However, when doing things outside of your comfort zone, you should try to expect everything possible.

- Another essential thing you need is to accept everything. Now don't get me wrong. I do not mean you should accept defeat whenever you face difficult situations. What I mean is that you should embrace difficult situations as a part of your growth process. Without a few difficulties, there cannot be growth.

- Be relentless: this means that you should imbibe the habit of perseverance. Without this, it won't take long for you to run back into your shell when you eventually leave your comfort zone. Whenever you are facing those challenges, do not back down because no one ever succeeded by giving up in the face of challenges. When coming out of your shell, you are not only disrupting the order you have created for yourself, you have also, inadvertently disrupted the order that others have created for themselves about you. Often, people are slow to accept change. That is why you see them discouraging you from doing this against your usual order because they are not just used to that side of you. So, if you let those discouraging comments get to you, you are missing out on a big chance to change your life.

These steps are all-inclusive. You cannot achieve leaving your comfort zone without engaging all of these. So, doing one and leaving out the other cannot help you successfully achieve that change you desire.

CHAPTER SIX

Growth: A way to move beyond your past.

According to John C Maxwell on The Law of Awareness from "The 15 Invaluable Laws of Growth", "To grow, you must know yourself: your strengths, weaknesses, your interests and opportunities. You must be able to gauge not only where you have been, but also where you are now".

"Acknowledging your growth is a way to move beyond your past. Growth is inevitable. But the question is, are you willing to grow? Or are you going to allow the experiences to stop you from living a fulfilled life? Yes, you may have been hurt, suffered rejection, but you have a choice to move past it. Someone once said to me,

"Eloho it is not that easy. You do not know what I have been through, I just cannot let it go. Is it that you cannot let it go or you do not want to let it go? You have the power within you, it all starts with the mind if you are willing to let go".

I had a choice to remain where I found myself in 2012 or move past it. A few of my friends asked about the significance of "Arise", the title of my first album and my morning show. I shared with them how in late 2012, after I had suffered from rejection, I found it hard to move on and was stuck in that place, for about 3 months feeling sorry for myself, having a pity party. And then it struck me. I knew deep down I could not be in that place forever so I found myself doing one of the things I love doing most, singing and listening to worship music. My eldest son says "I sing when I am sad, I sing when I am happy, I sing when I do not need to". Music is my safe place and through the experiences I had been through,

I knew I had to rise to be there for somebody else which led me to release my first studio album "Arise". I stepped out despite all I had been through, despite all my inadequacies, despite my fears, I knew I had to rise and shine, because somebody needed what I had; my imperfections, my mistakes, my challenges, my victories and successes could help somebody else.

I believe that every single experience has brought me to the place where I am today. If I had not been through all of that how could I help someone else who is going through a similar process. So, I have learnt to always ask what I need to learn from this situation rather than ask "Why me?"

Every experience you have been through is part of the plan, the good, the not so good. You may not like it, but it is part of the process and if you open up your heart there are so many things to learn from.

So regardless of all the limitations I had, or the excuses I could have given, I decided I was still going to show up, I would keep at it, whether I was receiving accolades or not. This was me, who at a previous point, always sought for approval. I now began instead to focus on providing value, inspiring people whether I received the praises or not. Of course, people began to notice, as consistency builds trust.

As human beings we all desire to be appreciated and acknowledged but when I stopped seeking it, the appreciation and celebration came, people began to recognize my efforts and the same people who turned their backs on me, the same people who rejected me and looked down on me, have all at one time or the other reached out to me.

You cannot grow beyond your past if you keep going over what had happened, how you were treated and how you did not deserve it. If you want to grow, you must be willing to let your past go, I know it is not easy but it is a process and that is why I am committed to helping women of faith break away from all those stereotypes to become the women they were destined to be.

Growth is the process of developing yourself until you reach your full potential, you evolve into exactly what you should be. Like I say I am still on a journey.

As you grow, you come to the point where all your actions are geared towards self-development and improvement, no matter what your past may have been like. If that potential exists in you, you will always be drawn to being a better version of yourself.

Personal growth or development is essential for every one of us. As you grow, you naturally become more passionate about everything you are involved in, and you seek to invest in yourself so that you are able to add value to others. At the heart of all I do is the desire to add value to the lives of the people I encounter, which is why I am up very early every Monday to Thursday morning on the radio inspiring someone to start their day right. It is also the same reason I am coaching women of faith and helping business owners and creatives with providing a strategy for their social media.

Growth creates some type of maturity that creates a sense of motivation and excitement to go for things and participate in activities you would usually avoid.

At this point, I would say it is pretty much evident why we need to grow. To become better obviously. Possibly, if I had not gone through the process of coaching, reading, and taking time to understand myself (which are all responsible for my growth), I would still find it difficult to appreciate, love, and embrace my authentic self with all my imperfections and complexities. I might not have had the opportunity to acquire all that I have now if not for growth, and even if I had the opportunity, who says I would have appreciated it. I probably still would not have appreciated it because I had not experienced growth, and I did not understand the value of what I had.

Why Do I Have a Past?

Our past is a reflection of the decisions and steps we had taken in accordance with the belief and understanding we had back then. We have a past because we evolved. We have a past because things changed. We have a past because we crossed the hurdle of unlearning. We have a past because it is an innate feature of growth.

This does not mean that our past is horrible, or everything we once did should be regarded with a nose scrunched up in disgust. In fact, I have made it a point in my life never to look back on my past with regrets as I believe it was all a part of the growth process.

Our past is the definition of all we were before we crossed the hurdle of unlearning. It might be good; it might be bad; it might keep you up at night. Or it might bring a smile to your face whenever you remember it. The point to take home is that it is a vital part of our growth process, and your past has no authority over you, except that which you allow. Like I always say; "You cannot change the past, but you can at least leave it alone"

Why Should We Acknowledge Growth?

Now that I see things differently, this means I am a changed person. Doesn't it? I can now walk around confident in my own skin irrespective of the differences that exists between myself and others. I have grown beyond someone who used to live in the past, who had the wrong perspective on things, to someone who has evolved and is now confident in situations. I am still growing, and my growth could be attributed to the fact that I allowed it. I have consciously and intentionally put myself in positions that caused this growth.

Acknowledging this change in myself has helped me understand why I used to see the world through the wrong lens. It was simple enough, I did not understand myself or value myself, and I had no intention to embrace myself. Recognizing that growth and all that it brings with it, the good, the bad, the ugly, and the leg straining hurdles are all a part of living. It is fundamental and denying that invariably is denying yourself life.

Also, acknowledging your growth and achievements creates positive energy and emotions around you, because it is not enough for you to just grow, it is highly essential that you recognize and appreciate yourself that you have moved beyond where you used to be, even if you have not gone as far as you would have expected. Acknowledging and celebrating your growth helps to improve self-respect, self-admiration, appreciation, happiness, and confidence.

I read from an article that some plants are known to grow negatively, you know, they grow downwards. Like plants' roots normally do. If what fertilizes your growth is of dubious source, you will grow but negatively like the roots. Not only is that counterproductive, but it is also disastrous.

Why Should We Acknowledge the Past?

Acknowledging that there was a period in my life where I felt like I was not good enough has helped me in my growth journey to be the woman I am destined to be. Knowing this helps me grow beyond the point where I am now. There is no limit to your growth, as long as you are intentional and are involved in the right activities.

The past should serve as a reminder of things that can turn out to be better than our beginnings and our predicted situations. Of course, there is the issue of the past that hurts. Not every scenario of what the past holds or held is hilarious and offhandedly comical. In fact, most of them are not. However, the ability to say to yourself, "Yes, I may have had a hurtful past, but I will not let it define me" is the key to success in this journey.

CONCLUSION

Stop doubting your potential and start living the awesome life you were created to live. I have shared my experiences and journey in this book and I do hope you find inspiration to rise and shine.

In your career, business or any situation you find yourself, never ever sell yourself short. It took me some time to conclude that if I can pay other people to get results, then others can pay me as well. If you do not place value on yourself no one else will.

Therefore, adopt/adapt the recommendations that are scattered all through this book to assist yourself on your journey to building confidence and embracing your unique self. Read books and review them, talk about the things you have learned to anyone that might listen. Surround yourself with people who celebrate you and push you to be the best version of you.

In my journey, I have come to the conclusion that I cannot be everything to everyone. I felt if everybody liked me, I would feel better, but that did not work. In fact, it only drained me and affected my self-esteem. The truth is that I cannot be everyone's cup of tea, maybe somebody's coffee or hot chocolate.

You are not everyone's cup of tea; you might not even be a cup of tea, but always remember that there is someone out there who loves hot chocolate. I choose to focus on these kinds of people, and you should too.

I have also chosen to focus on being a blessing to somebody else and stop seeking approval. Focusing on my assignment is my priority. What is this assignment that I have mentioned? What am I supposed to be doing in other people's lives? I focused on helping people. I have chosen to focus on my lane, and I spend most of my energy on positive things- trying to get clarity about my goals, dreams, and visions, which has helped me.

You may have suffered from a lack of confidence; you may have been beaten down, but if I can overcome it, then so can you. This journey to self-growth is a process and it takes time; do not rush it. Sometimes, I still battle with those thoughts, but my faith plays a huge and vital role in helping me stay focused.

This book is my story: Abused. Rejected. Disappointed. Low self-esteem. Inferiority complex, Lack of confidence, Mistakes. All of that has not stopped me and should not stop you either. Now, I am bold, fearless, I love me, I value myself and I am enjoying the process.

My sincere desire is that this book is of great inspiration to you in whatever stage of life you find it, or it finds you.

Embrace and celebrate your uniqueness, accept the fact that not everyone has to have a seat at your table, and you do not have to be at everyone's table.

To whoever is reading this, let this book be a reminder, that you are enough, you have enough, you do not need to add to it or fix it. You just need to believe in you more and grow yourself. You might not be the right flavor of tea or beverage choice for everyone, but you are still enough. People do not validate your completeness. let these words take root in your mind- YOU ARE NOT EVERYONE'S CUP OF TEA.

GET MY DAILY AFFIRMATIONS

When nobody else celebrates you, you've got to celebrate yourself. When no one believes you or believes in you, you've got to believe in yourself. When no one compliments you, compliment yourself. It's not up to anyone to keep you encouraged.

I regularly had to keep encouraging myself and celebrating myself. Little did I know that one day these same things I encouraged myself with I'd be encouraging others with a book. I have curated these positive affirmations to help you on your journey. Click the link to get them.

http://elohoefemuai.co.uk/daily-affirmation/

Here are some screen shots of how I affirmed and encouraged myself on my journey. I help they inspire you to come with yours.

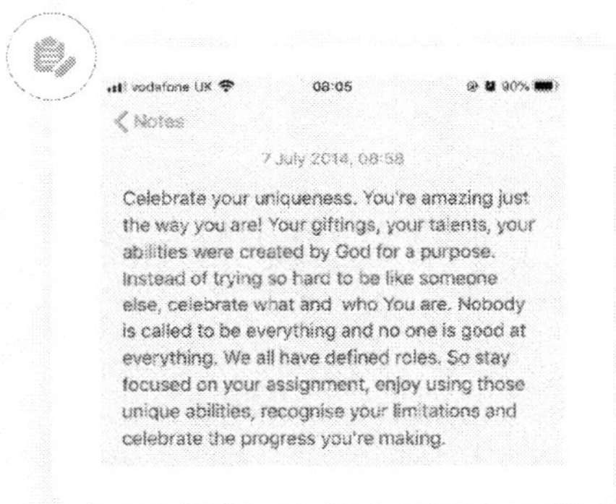

vodafone UK 08:02

< Notes

13 November 2013, 06:49

Quit comparing or trying to be like him or her! It's definitely easier to be You and do You! You're unique all by yourself! In all the world there can never be another You! You are the original version of You! The best version of You! You're so totally awesome! You were created to fulfil purpose! You were born for more! Don't settle for less! God loves You just the way You are!

vodafone UK 08:02

< Notes

23 October 2013, 09:24

Not everyone will like you or like your style! No matter what you do or don't do some people will not be impressed, so never change who you are for anyone.

vodafone UK 08:01 91%

< Notes

23 October 2013, 09:09

That gift/ talent God has blessed you with is not for you but for someone else! Someone needs to hear that message, listen to that song, read that book or story, and watch that movie! Someone needs that recipe book, that idea, that concept burning within you! The truth is that it may or may not reach the ends of the earth but it will reach someone within your circle of influence and change that life for good. Do not let your giftings and talents go to waste away or lie dormant. Someone needs it. So I encourage you to stir it up! It may not be everyone's cup of tea but may be someone's 'hot chocolate' or 'coffee' lol!

vodafone UK 08:02 91%

< Notes

6 November 2013, 08:22

People who will love you, will love you it doesn't matter what you do or don't do!

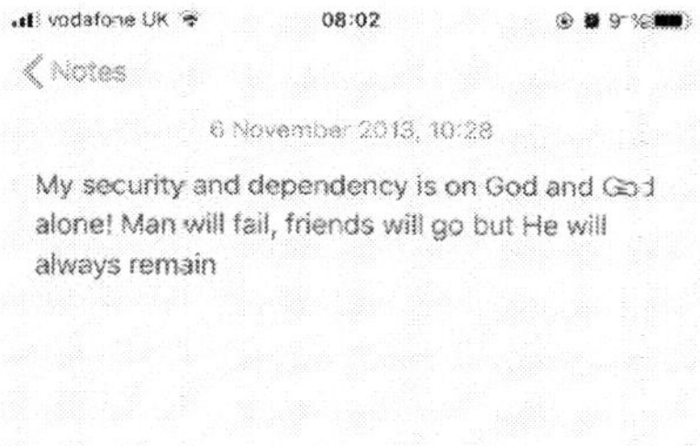
vodafone UK 08:02

< Notes

6 November 2013, 10:28

My security and dependency is on God and God alone! Man will fail, friends will go but He will always remain

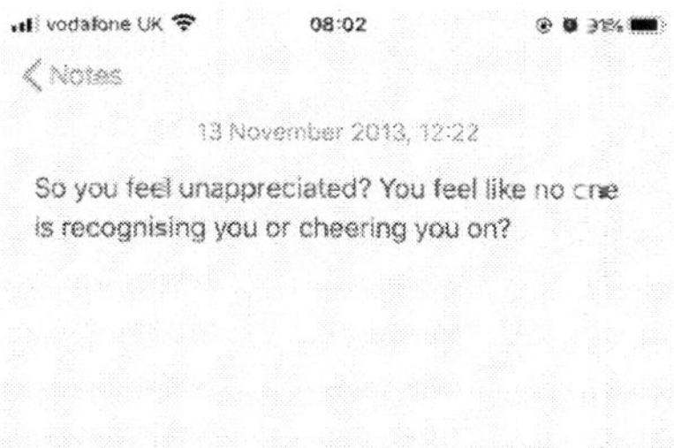
vodafone UK 08:02

< Notes

13 November 2013, 12:22

So you feel unappreciated? You feel like no one is recognising you or cheering you on?

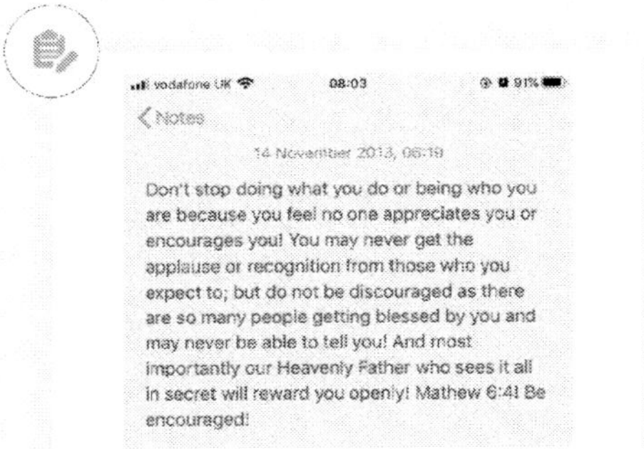

vodafone UK 08:03 91%

Notes

14 November 2013, 06:19

Don't stop doing what you do or being who you are because you feel no one appreciates you or encourages you! You may never get the applause or recognition from those who you expect to; but do not be discouraged as there are so many people getting blessed by you and may never be able to tell you! And most importantly our Heavenly Father who sees it all in secret will reward you openly! Mathew 6:4! Be encouraged!

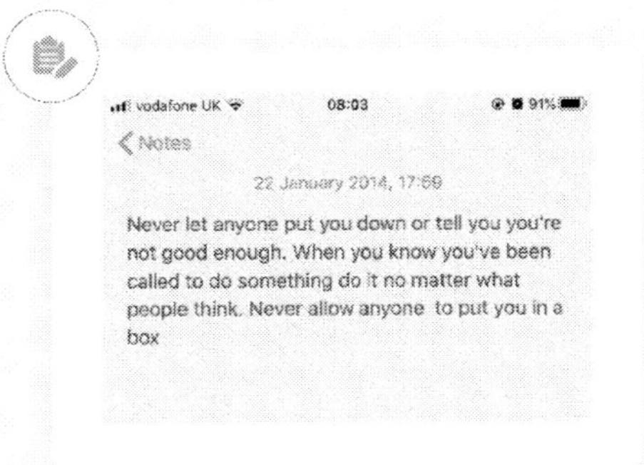

vodafone UK 08:03 91%

Notes

22 January 2014, 17:59

Never let anyone put you down or tell you you're not good enough. When you know you've been called to do something do it no matter what people think. Never allow anyone to put you in a box

YOUR NEXT STEPS

As we come to a conclusion, I would like to encourage you not to just read this book, get excited and then go back to living a life of low self-esteem and doubting your potential. You are good enough and have so much to offer. You cannot afford to go back to that place, you have a choice to stop doubting your potential grow yourself, take action and start to live the fulfilled life you were created to live.

You may still have some questions and would need some guidance with identifying what action steps you need to take, or you may require support in finding confidence.

If this is you, there are so many ways I would love to help and support you. However, to start off, I would love to invite you to join my online community "Arise Empowered" designed for those who struggle with their identity and a lack of confidence; those who need the support and motivation to become the very best version of themselves, to rise from whatever ashes and shine.

I know you will enjoy being a part of this community as there are others waiting to inspire you, hold you accountable and support you in every area of your life.

My desire is to see you live the life you were designed to live, whatever you do, I implore you to make a decision today that will move you forward. You were designed to shine. What you need now is the right skills and support.

If you need further information please send me an email at eloho@elohoefemuai.co.uk

NOTE FROM THE AUTHOR

THANK YOU

Thank you for buying my book. I would love this book to be read by as many people as possible because I believe it will transform their minds and set them free from living a life of low self-esteem.

If you enjoyed reading it, please help spread the word by doing the following

Recommend it- Suggest and share with others in your circle

Talk about it- Mention it across your social media platforms- Facebook, Instagram, Twitter or LinkedIn. You can start a conversation around it using hashtags #youarenoteveryonescupoftea #selfworthforwomen #ariseempowered. You may also use the cover image as your profile picture across your social networking sites

Write about it- Review it and write your thoughts in an article or a blog

Discuss it- Recommend it to your book clubs and discuss the chapters

Review it- Most importantly, leave a review on Amazon, when you do, Amazon is likely to suggest it to others.

As a thank-you I would like to give you the opportunity to win a FREE 30 minute discovery session to help you boost your self-esteem and build that business or brand that sets your soul on fire.

http://elohoefemuai.co.uk/discovery-session/

Just before you go, don't forget to get my list of daily affirmations. These affirmations are Bible based, but they help me daily and remind me of who I am and they will help you too.

http://elohoefemuai.co.uk/daily-affirmation/

Books that helped me

The 15 Invaluable Laws of Growth- John Maxwell

How Successful People Think- John Maxwell

Put Your dream to the test- John Maxwell

Today matters by John Maxwell

As a man thinketh- James Allen

Authentic- Ola Olaleye

5 Things successful people do before 5 am- Terri Savelle

The Miracle Morning- Hal Elrod

The One Thing-Gary Keller with Jay Papasan

Eat That Frog- Brian Tracy

Who Moved my Cheese- Dr Spencer Johnson

Start with Why- Simon Sinek

Becoming a person of influence- John Maxwell

REFERENCES

1. https://medium.com/thrive-global/3-reasons-why-you-shouldnt-look-for-validation-from-others-3823fea2c319

2. https://www.more-selfesteem.com/importance.htm

3. https://www.elitedaily.com/life/know-worth-little-ways-build-confidence/685031

Printed in Great Britain
by Amazon

44230269R00072